Graham Hicks' First Ever Joke Book

Graham Hicks' First Ever Joke Book

To order, please contact
Graham Hicks, Edmonton Sun
#250, 4990 - 92 Ave.
Edmonton, Alberta, Canada T6B 3A1
or
www.hicksonsix.com

PREFACE

A great tradition rules in Hicks on Six, the human interest column that runs five days a week on Page Six of the Edmonton Sun newspaper.

The column must start with a joke.

Other pages of the newspaper, of necessity, deal with murder and mayhem.

Hicks on Six provides relief, a chuckle, a guffaw, or if we're really lucky, a side-splitting laugh. The only way to start a day!

After thousands of requests for re-prints, and to raise money for the Edmonton Christmas Bureau, I'm proud to present Graham Hicks' First Ever Joke Book.

In these pages you'll find a selection of clean, funny and fresh jokes that have appeared on Page 6 of the Edmonton Sun in recent years.

Rest assured, you're not the only person who can't remember a good joke when you most need it. That's why the First Ever Joke Book is arranged by topics. Carry it with you at all times!

For new-comers to Hicks on Six and the Edmonton Sun, some insights.

Billy Bob and Skeeter are fictional stars of the column, two redneck pals from Edmonton's sister city of Calgary, Alberta. Billy Bob and Skeeter can be easily replaced by whoever you want as you re-tell these jokes.

You can't have a joke book without sections for blonds, lawyers and politicians. To all blond female lawyers turned politicians, we apologize in advance.

"Jokes for Special Days" is a section with jokes for festive days throughout the year, i.e. Christmas, Halloween etc.

This book ends on an affirmative note. "From The Heart" is a collection of short morality tales reminding us how sweet tears can be.

Enjoy these jokes. Feel free to tell them to all your friends.

Graham Hicks, Hicks on Six Columnist, The Edmonton Sun

ABOUT THE CHRISTMAS BUREAU

Two dollars from every copy of Graham Hicks' First Ever Joke Book will be donated to the Edmonton Christmas Bureau. The Christmas Bureau is a unique charity with a deep history in our city. It ensures no Edmontonian, no matter how old, or young, or down and out, goes without a Christmas holiday feast. Every Christmas, some 14,000 low-income families and singles in Edmonton receive a festive food hamper or grocery store gift certificates from this wonderful, simple charity.

ACKNOWLEDGEMENTS

The jokes in this book have almost all been passed on by joke-collecting Sun readers over the years. You are too numerous to mention by name, but thank you so much for sharing so much good humour.

The Edmonton Sun is a great partner in this endeavour, distributing and marketing this collection of jokes. To my colleague Barry Hanson, thank you for the editing and design, to Sun Photographer Perry Mah for the front-cover photograph, to Sun Art Director Tammy Wolfater for the front-cover design. Thanks to Rob Lelacheur for inspiring this book.

Thanks to my children Elizabeth, Rosalina and Cynthia – who critique the "Hicks on Six" joke every day. And to my wife Maria: Without her love, encouragement and understanding, I am nothing.

Contents

All In the Family

ABSENCE MAKES HIS HEART MUCH FONDER

A woman reported the disappearance of her husband to the police.

The officer looked at the photograph she handed him, questioned her and then asked if she wished to give her husband any message if they found him.

"Oh, yes," she replied. "Tell him my mother didn't come after all."

IMPROVES WITH YOUTH

A little girl was sitting with her grandfather as he read her a bedtime story.

From time to time she would take her eyes off the book and reach up to touch his wrinkled cheek.

She'd then touch her cheek, then touch his again.

Finally she spoke up, "Grandpa, did God make you?"

"Yes, sweetheart," he answered. "God made me a long time ago."

"Oh," she paused. "Grandpa, did God make me too?"

"Yes indeed, honey," he said. "God made you just a little while ago."

Feeling their respective faces again, she observed, "God's getting better at it, isn't he?"

WHAT MOM TAUGHT

MOM taught me TO APPRECIATE A JOB WELL DONE. "If you're going to kill each other, do it outside. I just finished cleaning!"

MOM taught me RELIGION. "You'd better pray this gunk comes out of the carpet."

MOM taught me LOGIC. "Because I said so, that's why."

MOM taught me FORESIGHT. "Wear clean underwear in case you're in an accident."

MOM taught me IRONY. "Keep crying and I'll give you something to cry about."

MOM taught me OSMOSIS. "Shut your mouth and eat your supper!"

MOM taught me CONTORTION. "Will ya look at the dirt on the back of your neck?"

MOM taught me STAMINA. "You'll sit there until all that spinach is finished."

MOM taught me HYPERBOLE. "If I've told you once, I've told you a million times. Don't exaggerate!"

MOM taught me BEHAVIOUR MODIFICATION. "Stop acting like your father!"

MOM taught me ENVY. "There are millions of less-fortunate children in this world who don't have wonderful parents like you do!"

MOM taught me THE CIRCLE OF LIFE. "I brought you into this world and I can take you out."

MOMS, YA GOTTA LOVE 'EM

You know you're a mom when ...

Your feet stick to grape jelly on the kitchen floor and you don't care.

You spend an entire week wearing nothing but sweats.

The baby's pacifier falls on the floor and you give it back to him/her after you suck the dirt off it because you're too busy to wash it off.

The kids make jokes about farting, burping, pooping, etc., and you think it's funny.

You're so desperate for adult conversation you spill your guts to the telemarketer, so much so that he hangs up on you.

Spit is your No. 1 cleaning agent.

You hide in the bathroom to be alone.

You're up at 5:30 every morning, not in bed until 11 at night. The time is spent vacuuming, dusting, wiping, washing, drying, loading, unloading, shopping, cooking, driving, flushing, ironing, sweeping, picking up, changing sheets, changing diapers, bathing others, helping with homework, paying bills, budgeting and folding clothes.

You've had no time to eat, sleep or drink. Yet you still gained 10 pounds last year.

MOTHER'S INTUITION

John invited his mother over for dinner to meet his roommate, Julie.

During the meal, his mother couldn't help but notice how beautiful she was. Mom started to wonder if there was more between John and his roommate than met the eye.

Reading mom's thoughts, John volunteered, "I know what you must be thinking, but I assure you, Julie and I are just roommates."

A week later, Julie asked John, "Have you seen the gravy ladle? It's been missing since your mom was here. You don't think she took it?"

John wrote a delicately worded e-mail to his mom.

Dear Mom, I'm not saying you took the gravy ladle from my house, I'm not saying you didn't. But the fact remains. It's been missing since you were here.

Mom wrote back.

Dear Son, I'm not saying you sleep with Julie. I'm not saying you don't sleep with her. But the fact remains. If she was sleeping in her own bed, she'd have found the gravy ladle by now.

THINGS YOU'LL NEVER HEAR DAD SAY ON FATHER'S DAY

10. Well, how about that? I'm lost! Looks like we'll have to stop and ask for directions.

9. You know, sweetheart, at 13 you should be ready for unchaperoned car dates.

8. I've noticed that you and all your friends have a certain hostile attitude. I like that.

7. Here's a credit card and the keys to my new car. GO CRAZY!!

6. You want to play football? Figure skating's not good enough for you, son?

5. Your mother and I are going away for the weekend. You might want to consider throwing a party.

4. Don't you worry about that exam tomorrow. You just talk to your friends on MSN as long as you like.

3. You know how much your mother loves your tongue split, nose rings and purple hair.

2. Your boyfriend wants to move in? Sure! You might as well share the same bedroom.

1. What do I want for Father's Day? Aahh - don't worry about me. It's no big deal.

ON BEING A PARENT

Shouting to make your children obey is like using the horn to steer your car. You get the same results.

Any child can tell you that the sole purpose of a middle name is so he can tell when he's really in trouble.

Best advice for raising children: Enjoy them while they're still on your side.

Life's golden age: When the kids are too old to need baby-sitters and too young to borrow the family car.

Raising a teenager is like nailing Jell-O to a tree.

Parents: People who bear infants, bore teenagers and board newlyweds.

Three ways to get things done: Do it yourself, hire someone to do it or forbid your children to do it.

Cleaning your house while your kids are at home is like trying to shovel the driveway during a snow-storm.

Alarm clock: A device for awakening people who don't have small children.

Out Of The Mouths Of Babes (About Kids)

PUSH, PULL, PUSH, PULL

With winter's arrival, a teacher was helping a kindergarten student put on his boots.

She pulled, he pushed.

They finally got both boots on.

"Teacher," the little boy said. "They're on the wrong feet."

She kept her cool. Together they put the boots on the right feet.

"Teacher," he said, "These aren't my boots."

She bit her tongue. Again the boots came off.

"Teacher," the child announced. "They're my brother's boots. My mom made me wear them."

She mustered what grace and courage she had left and wrestled the boots onto his feet again.

"Now," she said, "where are your mittens?"

"Teacher, I stuffed them in the toes of my boots."

Her trial is scheduled for next year.

THE ANSWER IS OBVIOUS

"If I gave all my money to the church, would that get me into Heaven?" the Sunday school teacher asked her children.

"NO!" the children answered in unison.

"If I cleaned the church every day, mowed the yard and kept everything tidy, would that get me into Heaven?"

"NO," came the chorus.

"If I was kind to animals, gave candy to all children and loved my husband, would that get me into Heaven?"

"NO!"

"Well, then," said the teacher, "what do I have to do to get into Heaven?"

A five-year-old boy shouted, "YOU GOTTA BE DEAD!"

THE FIRST CUT IS THE DEEPEST

Two children were alone in a doctor's waiting room.

The little girl was softly sobbing.

"Why are you crying?" asked the little boy.

"I'm here for a blood test. They're going to cut my finger," sniffled the girl.

When he heard this, the little boy started to cry.

"Why are you crying?" asked the girl.

The boy looked at her worriedly and said, "I'm here for a urine test."

CUTE WITTLE WABBITS

A little girl walks into a pet shop and asks in the sweetest little lisp, "Excuthe me, mithter. Do you keep wittle wabbits?"

The shopkeeper gets down on one knee so he can talk to her eye-to-eye. "Do you want a wittle white wabbit, or a soft 'n' fuwwy bwack wabbit?" he asks.

She, in turn, puts her hands on her knees, bends forward and says, "I don't fink my pyfon weally cares."

FOR THE SICK

A little girl was in church with her mother when she started feeling ill.

"Mommy," she whispered, "can we leave?"

"No," her mother replied.

"Mommy, I'm gonna be sick."

"Go out the front door and around to the back of the church," hissed her mom. "If you must, throw up behind a bush."

Just a minute later, the girl returned to her seat.

"Were you sick?" asked her mom quietly.

"Yes," she said.

"How could you have gone to the back of the church and returned so quickly?"

"I didn't have to leave the church. There's a box beside the door that says, 'For the Sick.' "

A POT AND A PRAYER

A young man visited his sister who had married a poor farmer.

As the house was small, he shared a bedroom with his young nephew.

Coming into the bedroom that night, he saw the young fella kneeling at the side of the bed with his head bowed.

Thinking the child was in prayer, he decided to follow his nephew's example.

He kneeled at the other side of the bed, bowed his head.

The boy glanced up. "Whatcha doing?" he asked.

"The same thing as you," replied his uncle.

"Mom's gonna be mad," said the boy. "The pot's on this side."

PREGNANT FIREFIGHTERS

"Write a sentence about anybody in the emergency services," the teacher instructed her young charges.

The small boy wrote: "A fireman came down the ladder pregnant."

The teacher took the lad aside to correct him.

"Do you know what pregnant means?" she asked.

"Yep," said the young boy confidently. "Means carrying a child."

Seniors' Moments

SENIOR'S LAMENT

I've had two bypass surgeries, a hip replacement, new knees, fought cancer and diabetes. I'm half blind, can't hear anything quieter than a jet engine.

I take 40 different medications that make me dizzy, winded, and subject to blackouts.

I have bouts with dementia, poor circulation, hardly feel my hands and feet anymore.

I can't remember if I am 68 or 86. All my friends are gone.

But, thank goodness, I still have my driver's licence!

SHARE A BITE

A young man is watching an old couple at a fast-food restaurant.

They've bought a combo meal with an extra glass.

The husband cuts the burger in half, divvies up the fries, pours half the soft drink into the extra cup.

His wife takes her half. While the old man eats, she waits, hands folded.

The young man, troubled, asks if he could buy the couple another meal so they didn't have to split.

"Oh no," the old gentleman said. "We've been married 50 years. We've shared everything, 50-50."

The young man asked the wife if she was going to eat.

"Not yet," she replied. "It's his turn with the teeth."

ALCOHOL'S NOT THE PROBLEM

The old gal's in a Scottish pub celebrating her 80th birthday.

"What will you have?" says the bartender as he buys her a drink.

"A double Glenfiddich (whisky) and two drops of water," she says.

Fella down the bar treats her as well.

"Double Glenfiddich and two drops of water," she says. And on it goes.

After her fifth double Glenfiddich and two drops of water, the barkeep has to ask. "Ma'am, why just two drops of water with each drink?"

"Sonny," she says. "At my age, I can still hold my liquor. But I just can't control my water."

DOUBLE-BARRELLED MEMORY BLANKS

Two elderly ladies had been friends for many decades.

Over the years they had shared all kinds of activities and adventures. Lately, their activities had been limited to meeting a few times a week to play cards.

One day they were playing bridge. One looked at the other one and said, "Don't get mad at me. I know we've been friends for a long time, but I just can't think of your name! I've thought and thought, but I can't remember it. Please tell me what your name is."

Her friend glared at her.

For at least three minutes she just sat and glared at her.

Finally she said, "How soon do you need to know?"

17

WHAT TO BUY FOR GRAMPS

Jacob, aged 92, and Rebecca, 85, are all excited about their decision to get married.

They're out for a stroll to discuss their marriage plans and happen to pass a drugstore.

Jacob suggests they go in.

"Do you sell heart medication?" Jacob asks the pharmacist.

"Of course," he replies.

"Medicine for circulation?"

"All kinds."

"Medicine for rheumatism?"

"Definitely."

"How about Viagra?"

"Of course."

"Medicine for memory?"

"We carry a large variety."

"Vitamins and sleeping pills?"

"Absolutely."

Jacob turns to Rebecca. "Sweetheart, we might as well register our wedding gift list with them."

LOW-TECH SOLUTIONS

Fella's shopping for a hearing aid.

"How much are they?" he asks the salesman.

"Anywhere from $2 to $2,000," says the salesman.

"Let's see the $2 model."

The salesman pulls out a button attached to a string.

"Stick the button in your ear, then run the string down to your shirt pocket."

"How can that possibly improve my hearing?"

"It doesn't," replies the salesman. "But when people see it on you, they'll talk louder."

How Women See The World

MEN: YA GOTTA LOVE US

What's the definition of macho? Jogging home from your own vasectomy.

What's the difference between a G-spot and a golf ball? A guy will actually search for a golf ball.

Why do men find it difficult to make eye contact? Breasts don't have eyes.

Why do most women pay more attention to their appearance than improving their minds? Because most men are stupid. But few are blind.

Why are married women usually heavier than single women? Single women come home, see what's in the fridge and go to bed. Married women come home, see what's in the bed and go to the fridge.

When do women really want a man's company? When he owns it.

How do you get a man to do situps? Tape the remote control between his toes.

HI HO, FOR THE LIFE OF A BEAR

The case for being a bear, if you're female.

If you're a bear, you get to hibernate. You do nothing but sleep for six months.

Before you hibernate, you're supposed to eat yourself stupid.

If you're a bear, you give birth to your children (who are walnut-sized) while you sleep. When you wake up, they're cute cuddly cubs.

If you're a mama bear, everyone knows you mean business. You swat anyone who bothers your cubs. If your cubs get out of line, you swat them, too.

Best of all, if you're a bear, your mate expects you to wake up growling. He expects that you will have hairy legs and excess body fat.

HE SAID, SHE SAID

He said: "Want a quickie?" **She said:** "As opposed to what?"

He said: "This coffee isn't fit for a pig!" **She said:** "No problem, I'll get you some that is."

She said: "What do you mean by coming home half-drunk?" **He said:** "It's not my fault. I ran out of money."

He said: "Why do women try to impress men with their looks, not with their brains?" **She said:** "Because there's a much greater chance a man will be a moron than that he will be blind."

He said: "What have you been doing with all the grocery money?" **She said:** "Turn sideways and look in the mirror."

Question: Should I have a baby after 35?
Answer: No. Thirty-five children is enough.
Q: When is the best time to get an epidural?
A: Right after you find out you're pregnant.
Q: I'm two months pregnant. When will my baby move?
A: With any luck, after he finishes college.
Q: What is the most common pregnancy craving?
A: For men to get pregnant.
Q: What is the most reliable method to determine a baby's sex?
A: Childbirth.
Q: The more pregnant I get, the more often strangers smile at me. Why?
A: Because you're fatter than they are.
Q: My wife is five months pregnant and so moody that sometimes she's borderline irrational.
A: So what's your question?
Q: My childbirth instructor says it's not pain I'll feel during labour, but pressure. Is she right?
A: Yes, in the same way that a tornado might be called an air current.
Q: Is there any reason I have to be in the delivery room while my wife is in labour?
A: Not unless the word "alimony" means anything to you.
Q: Is there anything I should avoid while recovering from childbirth?
A: Yes, pregnancy.
Q: Do I have to have a baby shower?
A: Not if you change the baby's diaper very quickly.
Q: Our baby was born last week. When will my wife begin to feel and act normal again?
A: When the kids are in college.

CHANGING PLACES

The man was complaining as he prayed. "Lord, I work so hard while my wife stays at home. Grant me one wish. Switch me with my wife.

"She's got it so easy at home. I want her to learn how tough a man's life is."

God listened. He granted the man his wish. The next morning the "new" woman woke up at dawn, made lunches, breakfast, woke up the kids, started a load of laundry, planned for dinner, drove the kids to school, filled up the car, went to the bank, the dry-cleaners and the grocery store.

By 1 p.m., he made the beds, started a second load of laundry, vacuumed and cooked rice. He visited his aging mother-in-law at the nursing home, helped at the school, brought the kids home and argued with them about cleaning up.

As soon as they were fed, he started the dish-washer, helped the children with homework, watched TV while ironing, bathed the children, put them to bed and read them a story. By 9 p.m., he was so tired he went to bed.

Of course, there was another duty. Somehow he managed to get it done and fell asleep.

The next morning he was again praying to God.

"Lord, I don't know what I was thinking. I beg you, please switch me back to myself."

Then he heard God's voice. "My dear son, of course I'll switch you back to yourself. But there's one minor detail. You will have to wait nine months. Last night you got pregnant."

THE RIGHT WAY TO MARK A BIRTHDAY

A man entered a stationery store and asked the clerk for a birthday-anniversary card.

The clerk replied, "We have birthday cards and we have anniversary cards. Why not take one of each?"

The man said, "You don't understand. I need a card for both. Today we are celebrating the 30th anniversary of my wife's 30th birthday."

SELF-ENHANCEMENT

Fella asked his wife what she liked best about him.

"My firm, trim, athletic body, or my astounding intellect?"

His wife replied: "Your sense of humour, dear."

How Men See The World

If you put a woman on a pedestal and try to protect her from the rat race, you're a male chauvinist. If you stay home and do the housework, you're a pansy.

If you work too hard, there's never time for her. If you don't work enough, you're a good-for-nothing bum.

If you mention she looks nice, it's sexual harassment. If you keep quiet, it's male indifference.

If you cry, you're a wimp. If you don't, you're an insensitive lout.

If you make a decision without consulting her, you're a chauvinist. If she makes a decision without consulting you, she's liberated.

If you like a woman to shave her legs and keep in shape, you're sexist. If you don't, you're unromantic.

If you try to keep yourself in shape, you're vain. If you don't, you're a slob.

If you buy her flowers, it's to make amends. If you don't, you're not thoughtful.

If you're proud of your achievements, you're full of yourself. If not, you're unambitious.

If she has a headache, she's tired. If you have a headache, you don't love her anymore.

If you want it too often, you're oversexed. If you don't, there must be someone else.

UNDERSTANDING MEN

Improving your relationship with your husband:

Ask for what you want. Subtle hints do not work. Strong hints do not work. Obvious hints do not work. Just say it!

Men don't remember dates. Mark birthdays and anniversaries on a calendar. Remind us frequently beforehand.

Crying is blackmail.

"Yes" and "No" are perfectly acceptable answers to almost every question.

If something a man says can be interpreted two ways and one way makes you sad or angry, we meant the other way.

Come to us with a problem only if you want help solving it. That's what we do. Sympathy is what your girlfriends do.

Anything said six months ago is inadmissible in an argument. In fact, all comments become null and void after seven days.

If you think you're fat, you probably are. Don't ask us. We will refuse to answer.

As we are not mind readers, our lack of mind-reading ability is not proof of how little we care about you.

If we ask what is wrong and you say "nothing," we will act like nothing's wrong. We know you are lying, but it is just not worth the hassle.

It is neither in your best interest nor ours to take the quiz together. No, it doesn't matter which quiz.

SINGLE BLACK FEMALE

"Single Black Female seeks male companionship.
Ethnicity unimportant. I'm a very good looking young girl who LOVES to play.

I enjoy walks in the woods, riding in your pickup truck, hunting, camping, fishing trips, cosy nights lying by the fire.

Candlelight dinners will have me eating out of your hand.

Rub me the right way and watch me respond.

I'll be waiting for you after work, wearing only what nature gave me.

Kiss me and I'm yours.

Call and ask for Daisy."

Over 150 men answered the ad, to find themselves talking to the SPCA about an eight-week-old black Labrador retriever.

UNDERSTANDING SCIENTISTS

An architect, an artist and a scientist were discussing the merits of a wife or a lover.

The architect opted for marriage, building a solid foundation for an enduring relationship.

The artist chose a lover because of the passion and mystery.

"I'd like both," said the scientist.

"If you have a wife and a mistress, they will each assume you're with the other woman.

"Then you can go to the lab and get some work done!"

DISTRACTED DRIVERS

Driving to the office this morning, I saw a woman driver doing 90 km-h while looking into the rear-view mirror to apply her lipstick.

She was so absorbed that she suddenly veered into my lane.

I was so scared that I dropped my electric shaver, which knocked the doughnut out of my other hand. In all the confusion of trying to straighten the car using my knees against the steering wheel, my cellphone was knocked away from my ear.

It fell into the coffee between my legs, which splashed, causing me immense pain.

Worst of all, I lost a terribly important business call.

Darned women drivers.

TEN THINGS MEN LOOK FOR IN A WOMAN

1.
2.
3.
4.
5.
6.
7.
8.
9.
10. Wow! Check out that figure!

BLAME IT ON MY SEX

Because I'm a man ...

When the car runs badly, I will stare at the engine as if I know what I'm doing. If another man shows up, I'll say, "I used to fix these things, but with all these computers ... " We will then drink beer.

I can purchase milk or bread, but I cannot be expected to find exotic items like cumin or tofu. For all I know these are the same thing. Never expect me to pick up anything for which "feminine hygiene product" is a euphemism.

There is no need to ask me what I'm thinking. The answer will be sex or sports, though I'll make up something else if you ask. So don't.

I do not want to visit your mother, have her visit us, talk to her when she calls or think about her any more than I have to. Whatever you got her for Mother's Day is OK, I don't need to see it. And would you pick up something for my mom, too?

You don't have to ask me if I liked the movie. Chances are if you're crying at the end of it, I didn't.

What you're wearing is fine. What you were wearing five minutes ago was fine, too. Either pair of shoes is fine. Your hair is fine. You look fine. Can we go now?

I will share equally in housework. You do the laundry, cooking, gardening, cleaning and dishes. I'll do the rest.

Till Death Do Us Part (Marriage)

SWEPT OFF THEIR FEET

Two brooms were hanging in the closet. After awhile, they decided to get married.

One broom was, of course, the bride broom. The other was the groom broom.

The wedding was lovely. At the wedding dinner, the bride broom leaned over and said to the groom broom. "I think I am going to have a little whisk broom!!!"

"Impossible!," said the groom broom. "We haven't even swept together!"

FOUR SECRETS TO A HAPPY MARRIAGE

1. It is important to find a man who works around the house, cooks and cleans and helps care for the kids, and who makes money.

2. It is important to find a man who loves to spend money on you and show you a good time.

3. It is important to find a man who is good in bed and who loves to have sex with you.

4. It is important these three men never meet.

CULTURAL DIFFERENCES

An Albertan was travelling in Europe and happened to meet an Englishman and a Frenchman in a bar.

They started talking about problems with their wives.

"I told my wife she would have to do her own cooking," said the Englishman.

"The first day I saw nothing. The second day I saw nothing. But on the third day she prepared a wonderful dinner."

"I told my wife she had to do her own shopping and cleaning," said the Frenchman.

The first day I saw nothing. The second day I saw nothing. But on the third day the house was spotless and the pantry was filled with groceries.

"I gave my wife the same notice," said the Albertan. "She would have to start doing the cooking, shopping and housework. The first day I saw nothing. The second day I still saw nothing. On the third day, I could see just a little bit out of my left eye."

QUITE THE FIRST FIGHT

Three weeks after her wedding day, Joanna called her minister.

"Reverend," she wailed, "Billy Bob and I have had an absolutely dreadful fight!"

"Calm down, my child," said the minister. "It's not half as bad as you think. Every marriage has its first fight."

"I know, I know!" said Joanna. "But what am I going to do with the body?"

WHAT A TREAT

Fella wakes up this morning, kisses his wife and starts getting out of bed.

"Don't bother, honey," says his wife. "This morning, I'm taking care of breakfast."

He just about jumps for joy. "You are? You mean it? You never help with breakfast! Then again, I'm always the first one up. Do I get breakfast in bed?"

"Sure," his wife said. "Long as you'll come down at first to make the toast and coffee."

Putting the bread in the toaster, he enquires, "What are we having for breakfast?"

Replies his wife: "Toast and coffee."

WHAT A WOMAN WANTS, GOD WANTS

Newly married men's oath:

I will never, ever, forget Valentine's Day, or our wedding anniversary.

I will share the remote control.

I will always do the yard work, take out the garbage and help clean around the house.

I will never, ever, criticize my wife's driving.

My wife is always, always right.

Battle Of The Sexes

OFT-USED STRATEGY

Two men are walking down the street, eating as they talk.

Suddenly one starts choking, grabbing at his neck. The other panics, yells for help.

A well-dressed, serious-looking woman in a blue business suit is sitting nearby.

She looks up, neatly folds her newspaper, gets up from her seat and calmly makes her way over to the choking man.

She takes him by the shoulders, then once! twice! three times! knees him in the groin.

The man convulses violently and coughs up the bone stuck in his throat.

The lady walks back to her seat without saying a word.

As soon as he's sure his friend is OK, the other man rushes over to thank her.

"I've never seen anything like that," he marvels. "You're fantastic! Are you a doctor?"

"No," the woman replies. "I'm a divorce lawyer."

BUNCH OF BULL

Man takes his wife to the cattle auction.

They're walking down by the bull pens, when they spot a series of signs.

The first one reads: This bull mated 50 times last year. "He mated 50 times," says the wife to her husband. "You could learn from him."

The next sign reads: This bull mated 65 times last year. "You could learn from this big fella too," nags the wife.

The last sign reads: This bull mated 365 times last year. "Wow," says the wife. "That's once a day. You could really learn from him."

Finally, the husband fires back. "Ask," he says, "if it was 365 times with the same cow?

PICTURE THIS

During an evening of cuddling, the young guy glanced away from his girlfriend.

Looking around the room, he noticed a framed picture of another man on a desk in the distance. Naturally, the guy began to worry.

"Is this your husband?" he inquired nervously.

"No, silly," she replied, snuggling up to him.

"Your boyfriend then?" he asked.

"No, not at all," she said, nibbling away at his ear.

"Well, who is he then?" demanded the bewildered guy.

Calmly, she replied, "That's me before the surgery."

THE WIFE ALWAYS WINS

A man and his wife were having some problems at home and were giving each other the silent treatment.

The next week, the man realized he would need his wife to wake him at 5 a.m. for an early morning business flight to Toronto.

Not wanting to be the first to break the silence and therefore be the loser, he wrote on a piece of paper, "Please wake me at 5 a.m."

In the morning the man woke up to find it was 9 a.m and he had missed his flight.

Furious, he was about to go and see why his wife hadn't awakened him, when he noticed a paper by the bed.

The paper said, "It's 5 a.m. Wake up!"

SILENCE IS GOLDEN

"What's the matter? You look depressed."

"I'm having trouble with my wife."

"What happened?"

"She said she wasn't going to speak to me for 30 days."

"But that ought to make you happy."

"It did, but today is the last day."

MOODS

MOODS OF A WOMAN:

An angel of truth and a dream of fiction,
A woman is a bundle of contradiction,
She's afraid of a wasp, will scream at a mouse,
But will tackle her boyfriend alone in the house.
Sour as vinegar, sweet as a rose,
She'll kiss you one minute, then turn up her nose,
She'll win you in rage, enchant you in silk,
She'll be stronger than brandy, milder than milk.
At times she'll be vengeful, merry and sad,
She'll hate you like poison, then love you like mad.

MOODS OF A MAN:

Horny. Hungry.

Pitfalls of Passion (Infidelity)

BITING, SUCKING, ALL OVER MY BODY

I lie on my bed, thinking about you.

I feel this strong urge to grab you and squeeze you, because I can't forget last night.

You appeared to me unexpectedly. What happened in my bed left me tingling.

You came from nowhere. Shamelessly, without reservation, you lay on my naked body.

You sensed my indifference. You started to bite my body without guilt or humiliation.

You drove me crazy while you sucked me dry.

Finally I went to sleep. When I woke up, you were gone.

I searched for you but to no avail. Only the sheets bore witness to the night's events.

My body still shows your marks, making it harder to forget you.

Tonight I will remain awake, waiting for you.

As soon as you appear I will quickly grab you. I won't let you go.

I will crush you with my passion ... YOU ROTTEN MOSQUITO!!!

BUGS IN THE BEDROOM

A woman was having an affair with an inspector from a pest-control company.

They were carrying on in the bedroom when her husband arrived unexpectedly.

"Quick," said the woman. "In the closet!"

In he went, naked as the day he was born.

The husband discovered the man in the closet. "Who are you?" he demanded.

"I'm from Bugs-B-Gone," said the exterminator.

"What are you doing in my closet?"

"I'm investigating a complaint about an infestation of moths."

"And where are your clothes?" asked the husband.

The man looked down at himself.

"Look!" he exclaimed. "Look at what those little bugs have done!"

CAREFUL WHO YOU ASK

Fella goes to a psychiatrist.

"Doc, help me. My wife is unfaithful to me. Every Friday night, she goes to O'Malley's bar and picks up men. In fact, she sleeps with anybody who asks her! I'm going crazy. What should I do?"

"Relax," says the doctor, "take a deep breath and calm down.

"Now tell me, where exactly is O'Malley's bar?"

MASKED MARAUDER

The couple were invited to a costume ball, but as the wife was not feeling well, she stayed home. Feeling better after a few hours, she got up, put on her costume and went off to find her husband at the party.

She saw him all right. In full costume he was flirting outrageously with other women.

As her hubby hadn't seen her costume, she decided to flirt with him too.

Of course he took the bait. Without revealing her identity, she teased him endlessly and took him off to a private room.

Then she melted away into the evening, drove home, went back to bed.

"How was the ball?" she asked sleepily - very curious about how her husband would respond.

"I didn't even go," he said. "I went off to Joe's house instead, for a quiet night of poker with the boys."

As she was mentally drawing up the divorce papers, he continued. "One of the guys at the poker table wanted to go to the ball, so I lent him my costume.

"When he came back . . . did he have tales to tell!"

BRINGING IT ALL BACK HOME

What happens if you play a country music record backwards?

Your dog comes back, your wife comes back, you quit drinking . . .

SUSPICIOUS MINDS

When Adam stayed out late for a few nights in the garden of Eden, Eve became upset.

"You're running around with other women," she told her mate.

"Eve, honey, you're being unreasonable. You're the only woman on earth!"

The quarrel continued until Adam fell asleep. He woke up with a recurring chest pain.

It was his darling Eve poking him vigorously about the torso.

"What do you think you're doing?" Adam demanded.

Said Eve, "I'm counting your ribs."

Food And Its Consequences

RATIONALIZING CHOCOLATE

Chocolate is a mix of cocoa and sugar. Cocoa comes from beans, sugar from sugar cane or beets. It stands to reason. Chocolate is a vegetable.

Chocolate contains nature's perfect food, milk. So chocolate is a health food.

Chocolate-covered raisins, cherries, orange slices and strawberries all count as fruit.

Chocolate can have preservatives. Preservatives make you look younger.

A nice box of chocolates can provide your total daily intake of calories in one place. Isn't that handy?

Remember, the opposite of "stressed" (stressed spelled backwards) is "desserts."

LOAVES AND FISHES ARE FINE, BUT WHERE'S THE BEEF?

Mother Teresa died and went to heaven.

God greeted her at the Pearly Gates.

"Art thou hungry, Mother Teresa?" asks God.

"I could eat," Mother Teresa replies.

God opens a can of tuna and reaches for a chunk of rye bread and they share it.

While eating this humble meal, Mother Teresa looks down into Hell and sees the inhabitants devouring huge steaks, lobsters, pheasants, pastries and wines.

Curious, but deeply trusting, she remains quiet.

The next day God again invites her to join Him. Again, the meal is tuna and rye bread. Once again, Mother Teresa can see the citizens of Hell enjoying the best of haut-cuisine.

The following day, another can of tuna is opened. She can't contain herself any longer.

"God, I am grateful to be in Heaven with you as a reward for the pious, obedient life I led on Earth," says Mother Teresa.

"But here in Heaven all I get to eat is tuna and a piece of rye bread. In that other place, they are eating like emperors. I just don't understand."

God sighs. "Let's be honest," he says. "For just two people, does it pay to cook?"

SPEAKING OF FAT

God gave man broccoli and cauliflower and spinach, green and yellow vegetables of all kinds, so man would live a long and healthy life.

But Satan created fast food. And fast food produced the 99-cent double cheeseburger.

The fast food clerk said to man, "You want fries with that?"

Man said, "Supersize them." And man gained pounds.

God said, "Try my crispy fresh salad."

But Satan created ice cream. And man gained pounds.

God said, "Hey, I sent you heart-healthy vegetables and olive oil in which to cook."

But Satan created meat portions so big they flopped over the sides of the platter.

Man gained pounds. His bad cholesterol went through the roof.

God created running shoes. Man resolved to lose the extra pounds.

But Satan created the TV remote control, so man would not have to work at watching two NHL playoff games at the same time.

So man watched others play hockey. Man gained pounds.

God brought forth the potato, a vegetable naturally low in fat and brimming with nutrition.

But Satan created potato chips and sour-cream dip.

And man clutched his remote control and ate the potato chips swaddled in cholesterol.

Yummy! But man went into cardiac arrest.

God created quadruple bypass surgery.

Here endeth the cycle.

Even God could not afford the health bill!

TO ALL A GOOD DIET

'Twas the month after Christmas,
And all through the house
Nothing fit, not even a blouse.
The cookies I'd nibble, the eggnog I'd taste
At holiday parties had gone straight to my waist.
When I got on the scales there arose such a number.
When I walked to the store (less a walk than a lumber),
I'd remember the marvellous meals I'd prepared:
The gravies, sauces, beef nicely rared,
The wine and rumballs, bread and cheese
I never once said, "No thank you, please."
As I put on my husband's big old shirt
And prepared again to do battle with dirt
I said to myself, as I only can
'You can't spend all winter disguised as a man!'
Away with the last of the sour cream dip,
Get rid of the sweets, each cracker and chip.
Every bit of food I like must be banished
Till all additional ounces have vanished.
I won't have a cookie, not even a lick.
I'll only chew on a thin celery stick.
I won't have hot biscuits, cake or pie,
I'll munch on a carrot and quietly cry.
Unable to giggle, no longer a riot,
I'm hungry, I'm lonesome, life is a bore
But that's exactly what January is for.

INNER PEACE

My psychotherapist told me a way to achieve inner peace was to finish things I had started.

So yesterday I finished two bags of potato chips, a lemon pie, a case of beer and a small box of chocolate candy.

I feel better already.

NO PAIN IS GOOD FOR YOU

An interview with the revolutionary "health" practitioner Dr. Feelgood:

Q: Doc, will cardiovascular exercise prolong my life?

A: Your heart is only good for so many beats. Don't waste them on exercise. Speeding up your heart will not make you live longer. That's like saying you can extend the life of your car by driving it faster. If you want to live longer, take a nap.

Q: Should I cut down on meat and eat more grain, fruits and vegetables?

A: What does a cow eat? Hay and corn. And what are those? Vegetables. A steak is nothing more than an efficient mechanism for delivering vegetables to your system.

Need grain? Eat a chicken.

Q: Is beer or wine bad for me?

A: My point about vegetables. Everything comes in three categories, animal, mineral, and vegetable. Beer and wine are not animals or minerals. Have a burger and a beer and enjoy your liquid veggies.

Q: How can I calculate my body/fat ratio?
A: If you have a body and you have body fat, your ratio is one to one. If you have two bodies, your ratio is two to one, etc.

Q: What are the advantages of a regular exercise program?
A: None that I can think of. My philosophy is "No Pain Is Good For You."

Q: If I stop smoking, will I live longer?
A: No. Smoking is a stress reducer, unless you're trying to quit. Try to quit, you'll stress yourself to an early grave. Not to mention the pounds you'll put on.

Q: Aren't fried foods bad for you?
A: You're not listening. Foods are fried in vegetable oil. How could getting more vegetables be bad for you?

Q: Will situps prevent me from getting soft around the middle?
A: Definitely not! When you exercise a muscle, it gets bigger. Only do situps if you want a bigger stomach.

I hope this has cleared up any misconceptions you had about rigorous exercise.

Just One More Drink

GREY CUP WEEKEND, RSVP

Starkle, starkle little twink,
Who the heck you are I think.
I'm not under what you call
The alcofluence of incohol.
I'm just a little slort of sheep
I'm not drunk like tinkle peep.
I don't know who is me yet
But the drunker I stand the longer I get.
So just one more drink to fill me cup
'Cuz I got all day sober to Monday up.

INVESTIGATIVE SCIENCE

Four worms were placed into four jars. In each jar
was a different substance. One was filled with alcohol, the next cigarette smoke, the next used condoms, and finally soil.

After 24 hours, the worms in the alcohol, cigarette
smoke and condoms were dead.

The fourth worm in the soil was alive.

Which proves the following:

As long as you drink, smoke and have sex, you
won't get worms.

CRUNCHY MUNCHY GOLDEN OLDIE

Fella walks into a bar, orders a beer. He hears a soothing voice. "Nice tie."

He looks around. The bar is empty but for him and the bartender.

A few sips later the voice says, "Beautiful shirt."

"I must be losing my mind," the fella says to the bartender. "I keep hearing voices saying nice things, and there's not a soul in here but us."

"It's the peanuts," says the bartender. "They're complimentary."

A BEER BY ANY OTHER NAME

After a world beer festival, the brewery presidents go out for a beer.

"Senor bartender," says the Corona man. "I'll have Mexico's finest, a Corona."

Orders the Budweiser president: "Nothing but the best, the King Of Beers, a Bud."

The Coors man pipes up. "The only American beer brewed from Rocky Mountain spring water please, a cool, tasty Coors."

The Molson president arrives and motions to the bartender. "Get me a Coke."

The other brewery men are astonished. "Why aren't you drinking a Molson?"

"Well," he shrugs. "I figured if you guys aren't drinking beer, neither would I."

ALWAYS ROOM FOR A GOOD BREW

A philosophy professor had just been through the exercise of filling a large jar, first with rocks, then with pebbles, then sand.

The full jar had a moral, the professor said. Each material symbolized something.

The rocks were what really counted, family, partner, health, children.

The pebbles were other things that mattered - job, house, car, hobbies, etc.

The sand was everything else - the small stuff.

"You put the sand in first," said the prof. "You leave no room for the pebbles or rocks. Your time and energy is consumed by small stuff." Whereupon the good prof launched into a dissertation on spending one's time wisely on the big stuff.

One student, however, came to the front of the class carrying a bottle of beer.

He proceeded to pour the beer into the rocks, pebbles and sand, and into the jar which the others and the prof agreed was full.

"The true moral of this tale," said the student: "No matter how full your life is, there is always room for BEER!"

ADVICE FROM THE PROS

If you bought $1,000 worth of Nortel stock, it would be worth $50 today.

If you bought $1,000 worth of Molson or Labatt (the beer, not the stock) one year ago, drank it all and then took the bottles in for a refund, you'd have the same amount: $50.

My broker's advice: Start drinking heavily.

He Shoots, He Scores! (Sports)

MILK OF MAGNESIA

One football game, three of the moms of the players were watching in the stands.

The running back made a great play from a hand-off, 80 yards for a touchdown.

"That's my boy," said his mom. "I raised him on Carnation."

The fullback thundered through the line and carried five defensive players on his back 10 yards into touchdown territory.

"That's my son," said his mom. "I raised him on Dairyland."

With a minute left in the close game, the quarterback ran with the ball, slipped by the opposing linebackers, deked out the safety and had nothing but air between himself and the goal-line.

Then he stumbled, fell, and fumbled the ball.

"That's my boy," said his mom. "I raised him on Milk of Magnesia. Still as loose as ever."

2002 GREY CUP Q & A

(FOR FUTURE YEARS, INSERT YOUR FAVOURITE TEAMS, COACHES, PLAYERS BEFORE THE BIG GAME)

Q. Why was the coach upset when the Alouette's playbook was stolen?

A. He hadn't finished colouring it.

Q. How many Alouettes does it take to win a Grey Cup?

A. Nobody knows and we may never find out!

Q. What do you call 60 people sitting around a TV watching the Grey Cup?

A. The Winnipeg Blue Bombers.

Q. What do the Alouettes and possums have in common?

A. Both play dead at home and get killed on the road.

Q. How can you tell when the Alouettes are going to run the football?

A. Halfback Lawrence Phillips leaves the huddle with tears in his eyes.

Q. What's the difference between the Alouettes and the al-Qaida?

A. The al-Qaida have a running game.

Q. How do the Alouettes count to 10?

A. 0-1, 0-2, 0-3, 0-4, 0-5, 0-6, 0-7, 0-8, 0-9, 0-10.

Q. How do you keep a Montreal Alouette out of your yard?

A. Put up goal posts.

Q. Where do you go in Montreal in case of a tornado?

A. Molson Stadium. They never get a touchdown there!

Q. What do you call an Alouette with a Grey Cup ring?

A. A thief.

MAPLE LEAFS FOREVER (DENIED)

Two guys from Toronto die and go to hell.

The devil is surprised to see them dressed for winter, warming themselves by the fire.

"Isn't it hot enough for you?" the devil asks.

"We're from Canada, eh?" one replies. "The land of snow and ice and cold. We're happy just to warm up."

Deciding they weren't miserable enough, the devil turned up the heat.

The next morning, they were still dressed in parkas. "We told you," the Torontonians said. "Canada's so cold, we're just happy to be warming up."

The devil cranks the heat as high as it will go, goes off to find the Canadians in light jackets and ball caps, grilling burgers, drinking beer. "In Toronto when we get weather this nice we just have to have a cookout," says one.

Only one way to make these dudes miserable, the devil thinks to himself. He turns the heat off and the cold on.

The next morning, the temperature in hell is below zero. People are shivering so bad their teeth are falling out.

The devil can't wait to see the two Torontonians suffering.

Instead, he finds them jumping up and down, cheering, yelling and screaming like madmen!

"What?" says the devil. "I turn up the heat, you're happy. It's freezing. you're still happy. What is it with you two?"

The Torontonians look at the devil with surprise.

"You don't know?" shouts one. "When hell freezes over, it means the Leafs have won the Stanley Cup!"

FOOTBALL GROANER

A guy took his blond girlfriend to a football game for the first time.

After the game he asked her how she liked the game. "I really liked it," she said, "but I couldn't understand why they were killing each other for 25 cents."

The boyfriend looked puzzled. "What on earth do you mean???"

"Well, I saw them flip a coin.

"One team got it and then for the rest of the game the other team kept screaming, 'Get the quarter back! Get the quarter back!' "

LIGHT BULB LOSING

Q. How many soccer fans does it take to change a light bulb?

A. Seven - one to change it, five to moan about it and the coach to say that if the ref had done his job in the first place, the light bulb would never have gone out.

DREAM ON

A father called in his son.

"It's time we had a little talk, Junior.

"Soon you will have urges and feelings you've never had before.

"Your heart will pound. Your hands will sweat.

"You'll be preoccupied and won't be able to think of anything else.

"But don't worry, it's perfectly normal. It's called golf."

ALL EMOTION

In a class on abnormal psychology the instructor was about to introduce the subject of manic depression.

She posed this question to her students: "How would you diagnose a patient who walks back and forth screaming at the top of his lungs one minute, then sits in a chair weeping uncontrollably the next?"

A young man raised his hand and suggested earnestly, "A basketball coach?"

Pastors And Priests (Religious)

TOOT 'N' TELL

An elderly priest was complimenting the younger priest on his newfangled marketing ideas.

"When you replaced the first four pews with theatre seats, it worked. The front of the church is filling up first.

"Then you told me to add more of a beat to the music. You were right. The young people are back. We're packed.

"But," continued the elderly priest, "I'm afraid you've gone too far with the drive-through confessional."

"But Father," protested the young priest. "My confessions have nearly tripled since I started that."

"I know, my son," replied the old man. "But that flashing neon sign, 'Toot 'n' Tell or Go to Hell' can't stay on the church roof!"

NO COVERS

The Sunday school class was studying the Ten Commandments and they were ready to discuss the last one. The teacher asked if anyone could tell her what it was.

Susie raised her hand, stood tall and quoted, "Thou shall not take the covers off thy neighbour's wife."

DELIVER US E-MAIL

The dad had been teaching his two young children The Lord's Prayer.

At bedtime, he'd go over it with them, making them repeat the lines after him.

Finally it was time for each to go solo.

The three-year-old daughter carefully enunciated her words. "Lead us not into temptation," she prayed, "but deliver us some e-mail. Amen."

Prayed his four-year-old son: "And forgive us our trash baskets. As we forgive those who put trash in our baskets."

A POT TO POUR FROM

A nun is driving by herself when she runs out of gas.

She walks to the nearest town.

"I can get some gas for you, sister," says the gas station owner. "But I have no gas cans. They always get stolen."

He rummages around his personal quarters above the shop, and emerges with a child's pottie.

They fill it with gasoline. The nun hikes back to her car, carefully carrying the gas-filled pottie.

Just as she's pouring the contents of the pottie into her gas tank, an RCMP patrol car happens by.

The constable looks, rolls down his window.

"Sister," he says. "I sure admire your faith!"

HUSHED AND REVERENT

The mommy was telling her young children how to behave once they were in church.

"And why is it necessary to be quiet in church?" she asked them.

Replied her daughter, "Because people are sleep-ing?"

BIBLICAL KNOCK

A new preacher went to visit a well-known member of the congregation.

Somebody was obviously at home, but nobody came to the door.

The preacher took out his calling card, wrote on the back "Revelation 3:20," and left it in the mailbox.

The next Sunday, he found the parishioner's business card in the collection plate, with the notation "Genesis 3:10."

Revelation 3:20: "Behold, I stand at the door, and knock: If any man hear my voice, and opens the door, I will come in to him, and will dine with him, and he with me."

Genesis 3:10: "And he said, I heard thy voice in the garden, and I was afraid, because I was naked; and I hid myself."

Doctor Doctor, Tell Me The News

PLAN AHEAD

Mr. Jones phoned the doctor for an appointment.

The nurse said she could give him an appointment in six weeks.

"Six weeks!" wailed Mr. Jones. "By then I could be dead!"

"In which case," answered the nurse, "you could always cancel the appointment."

SEE THE DOCTOR

Lady tells her husband, "I keep seeing spots in front of my eyes."

"That could be serious," he says. "Have you seen a doctor?"

"No," she says. "Just spots."

SORRY ABOUT THE DELAY

Surrounded by friends and family, old Fred was fast fading on his hospital bed.

Suddenly, he motioned frantically to the pastor for something to write on.

The pastor lovingly handed him a pen and a piece of paper.

Fred used his last bit of energy to scribble a note, then fell back unconscious and promptly slipped from this world to the next.

As Fred had just died, the pastor thought it inappropriate to read the note at the time. Instead, he discreetly tucked the piece of paper into his jacket pocket.

During Fred's funeral a few days later, the pastor was delivering the eulogy.

He suddenly realized his jacket was the same he'd worn when Fred passed on.

"Fred handed me a note just before he died," the pastor said to the mourners. "I haven't looked at it, but knowing Fred, I'm sure there's inspiration in it for us all."

Opening the note, the pastor began reading out loud.

"'Help! You're standing on my oxygen tube!'"

ALARMING EXERCISE REGIME

I've started an exercise program.

I do 20 situps each morning.

That may not sound like a lot, but you can only hit that snooze button so many times.

BIG BREATHS

At the beginning of his shift, the doctor placed his stethoscope on an elderly and slightly deaf female patient's chest wall.

"Big breaths," he instructed.

"Yes," sighed the patient, "They used to be."

THE GOOD NEWS

The new doc wasn't sure how to break the news to the patient he didn't know very well.

He took a deep breath. "I have good news and bad news," he said.

"The good news is that you aren't a hypochondriac."

Pick On Politicians

FINAL PHOTO CALL

Three dead bodies turn up at the morgue, all with great big smiles on their faces.

The head coroner calls the police to check out this phenomenon.

The head detective arrives and inspects the first body. "Frenchman, 60, died of heart failure whilst making love to his mistress ... hence the enormous smile."

He checks the second body. "Scotsman, 25, won a lottery. Died from alcohol poisoning, but caused by the very best whisky. Hence the smile."

The detective pulls back the sheet on the third one.

"Ah," he says, "I recognize this fellow. It's the mayor. Struck by lightning."

"But why would he be smiling?" asks the coroner.

Replies the detective: "He thought he was having his picture taken."

NOT MUCH MISSED

The politician was the featured speaker at the local club's annual do.

However, the boys got down to some hard drinkin' before and during the meal.

It got so noisy that when the politician spoke, his voice could hardly be heard above the fray.

After, the politician stormed up to the club president. "It was so noisy in here, I could hardly hear myself speak."

"Never mind," the president reassured him. "You didn't miss anything."

JUST CAN'T TRUST WHAT THOSE POLITICIANS SAY

A busload of provincial politicians are driving by a farm where a man lives alone.

The bus driver, caught up in the beautiful Alberta scenery, loses control and crashes into the ditch.

The man comes out and, finding the politicians, buries them.

The next day, the RCMP are at the farm questioning the man.

"So you buried all the politicians?" asks the officer. "Were they all dead?"

The man answers, "Some said they weren't. But you know how politicians lie."

SOILED DIAPERS

What do baby diapers and politicians have in common?

They both need to be changed regularly - for the same reason.

POLITICS: THE RULES

If it's worth fighting for, it's worth fighting dirty for.

Don't lie, cheat or steal ... unnecessarily.

There is always one more SOB than you counted on.

An honest answer can get you into a lot of trouble.

The facts, although interesting, are irrelevant.

If you can't counter the argument, leave the meeting.

NO EGO AT ALL

Former prime minister Brian Mulroney, NDP leader Alexa McDonough and Canada's fearless leader Jean Chretien all die and turn up together at the Pearly Gates.

There they find God sitting on his throne.

God turns to Mulroney and asked what he believes in. "I believe in free trade and the GST," said Brian.

"Fine," God says, "Come sit at my right side."

God then asks McDonough what she believes in.

"I believe in medicare and helping the homeless."

"Fine," God said. "Come sit on my left side.

"And now, Mr. Chretien, what do you believe?

Replies Jean, "I believe you are sitting in my chair."

Gotta Have Lawyer Jokes

LAWYER SIGNS THE DEAL

A Mafia godfather discovers an underling has cheated him out of $10 million.

The underling happens to be deaf, so the godfather brings along a lawyer who knows sign language.

The godfather asks the henchman, "Where's the 10 million bucks you took from me?"

The attorney, using sign language, asks the underling where the 10 million dollars is.

The underling signs back, "I don't know what you are talking about."

The attorney tells the godfather, "He says he doesn't know what you're talking about."

The godfather pulls out a pistol, puts it to the man's head and says, "Ask him again!"

The attorney signs to the underling, "He'll kill you for sure if you don't tell him!"

The underling signs back: "OK! You win! The money is in a brown briefcase buried behind the shed in the backyard of my cousin Gus."

"What'd he say?" demands the godfather.

The attorney replies, "He says you don't have the guts to pull the trigger."

JUST A REGULAR LAWYER

Two small boys not yet in school met for the first time.

"My name is Billy. What's yours?" asked the first.

"Tommy," replied the second.

"My daddy's an accountant," said Billy. "What does your daddy do?"

Tommy replied, "My daddy's a lawyer."

"Honest?" asked Billy.

"No, just the regular kind," replied Tommy.

JUST A SUGGESTION

A redhead was thrilled to have obtained a divorce and dazzled by the skill and virtuosity of her lawyer, not to mention his healthy income and good looks.

In fact, she had fallen head over heels in love, even though he was a married man.

"Oh, Sam," she sobbed at the conclusion of the trial. "Isn't there some way we can be together, the way we were meant to be?"

Sam proceeded to paint out a future.

"Snatched drinks in grimy bars on the edge of town, lying on the phone, hurried liaisons in sordid motel rooms ... is that really what you want for us?"

"No, no," she sobbed, heartsick.

"Oh," said the lawyer. "Well, it was just a suggestion."

JURY DUTY

A man was chosen for jury duty who very much wanted to be dismissed from serving. He tried every excuse he could think of but none of them worked.

On the day of the trial, he asked if he could approach the bench.

"Your Honour," he said, "I must be excused from this trial because I am prejudiced against the defendant.

"I took one look at the man in the blue suit with those beady eyes and that dishonest face and I said 'He's a crook! He's guilty, guilty, guilty.' So your Honour, I could not possibly stay on this jury!"

"Get back in the jury box," said the judge. "That man is his lawyer."

BRIEF LEGAL MEETING

Two lawyers were walking along, negotiating a case.

"Look," said one to the other, "let's be honest with each other."

"Okay, you first," replied the other.

That was the end of the discussion.

Unfair to Blonds (but funny!)

BLOND CONFRONTATION

Fella was doing his ventriloquist act one night, starting a dumb blond joke with the dummy on his knee.

A blond in the audience exploded.

"I've heard enough of your stupid blond jokes!" she yelled. "How can you stereotype women that way?

"What does the colour of a person's hair have to do with her worth as a human being?

"Guys like you keep women like me from being respected! You stop us from reaching our potential as human beings!

"You and your kind perpetuate discrimination, not only against blonds but women in general. All in the name of humour!"

The performer began to respond when the blond cut him off.

"You stay out of this," she snarled. "I'm talking to that little jerk sitting on your knee!"

GOD WORKS WITH BLONDS

A blond is in serious trouble.

Her business has gone bust. She's in financial straits.

She asks God for help. "God," she prays. "Please help me. If I don't get some money, I'm going to lose my house as well. Please let me win the lotto."

Lotto night comes, and somebody else wins it.

Again she prays. "God, pleeeeze let me win the lotto. I've lost my business, my house and I'm going to lose my car."

Lotto night comes and she still has no luck.

On her knees, she wails, "My God, my God, why have You forsaken me? I've lost my business, my house and my car. The children are going hungry. I need your help. PLEASE let me win the lottery just this one time."

With a blinding flash of light the heavens open. The blond is overwhelmed by the voice of God Himself.

"Sweetheart, work with Me on this ... Buy a ticket!"

FEW DAYS LATE

How do you get a blond to laugh on Sunday?
Tell her a joke on Friday.

HELPFUL (BLOND) HEATHER

As a trucker stops at a red light, a blond catches up.

She jumps out of her car, runs up to his truck, and knocks on the door.

"Hi," she says. "My name is Heather and you are losing some of your load."

The trucker ignores her and proceeds down the street.

Another red light. Same thing. As if they've never spoken, the blond says brightly, "Hi! My name is Heather, and you are losing some of your load!"

The trucker ignores her again and continues on his way.

At the third red light, the same thing.

But as the truck rumbles to the next red light, the trucker quickly stops, gets out of his truck and runs back to the blond's car.

He knocks on her window. As she lowers it, he says, "Hi, my name is Kevin, it's winter in Alberta and I'm driving the SANDING TRUCK!"

PUZZLE WITH CRUNCH

In tears, the blond calls her boyfriend.

"Help! I've got this jigsaw puzzle I just can't figure out."

The boyfriend dutifully drives over, to find the pieces strewn all over a table. "Look," she sobs, "according to the box, it's supposed to be a tiger."

He looks at the box.

"Honey, no matter what we do, we won't assemble these pieces into anything resembling a tiger."

"Second, relax, have a cup of coffee, then we'll put all these Frosted Flakes back in the box."

GIVE HER A CHANCE

Some 80,000 blonds are gathered at a stadium for the "Blonds Are Not Stupid" convention.

"We are here to prove blonds are not stupid," says the leader. "Can I have a volunteer?"

A blond leaps on the stage.

"What is 15 plus 15?" the leader asks.

After 15 or 20 seconds, she says, "18?"

Everyone is disappointed, but 80,000 blonds shout "Give her another chance! Give her another chance!"

"OK," says the leader. "What's five plus five?"

After 30 seconds she guesses. "90?"

The blond starts crying. The 80,000 girls again chant "Give her another chance! Give her another chance!"

"Last chance," says the leader. "What's two plus two?"

The girl closes her eyes, and after a whole minute eventually says "Four?"

All 80,000 girls jump to their feet, wave their arms, stomp their feet and scream "GIVE HER ANOTHER CHANCE! GIVE HER ANOTHER CHANCE!"

WHO'S THE MOTHER?

What did the blond ask her doctor when he told her she was pregnant?

"Is it mine?"

THEY'LL NEVER GET IT

A blind man and his guide dog enter a bar and find their way to a bar stool.

After ordering a drink, the blind guy yells to the bartender, "Wanna hear a blond joke?"

A deathly hush falls over the bar.

In a husky, deep voice, the woman next to him says, "Before you tell that joke, you should know something.

"The bartender is blond, the bouncer is blond. I'm a six-foot-tall, 200-pound blond with a black belt in karate. What's more, the woman next to me is blond and she's a weightlifter.

"The lady to your right is a blond, and she's a pro wrestler. Think seriously, Mister. You still wanna tell that joke?"

The blind guy says, "Heck no! Not if I have to explain it five times!"

YELLOWED PAGES

The blond stormed into the public library.

"I have a BIG complaint!" she yelled.

"And that would be ..." asked the librarian at the front desk.

"I borrowed a book last week and it was horrible!"

"And what was wrong with the book?"

"It had way too many characters and there was no plot whatsoever!"

"Ahh," said the librarian knowingly. "You must be the person who took our phone book."

Canadian, eh? (Regional)

1. One hand on wheel, one hand on horn:
MONTREAL.

2. One hand on wheel, one finger out window:
TORONTO.

3. One hand on wheel, one finger out window, cutting across all lanes:
OTTAWA.

4. One hand on wheel, one hand on newspaper, cradling cellphone, balancing Tim Horton coffee on knee, foot solidly on accelerator:
CALGARY.

5. One hand on wheel, one hand on non-fat double decaf cappuccino, cradling cellphone, brick on accelerator, gun on lap:
LOS ANGELES.

6. Both hands on wheel, eyes shut, both feet on brake, quivering in terror:
REGINA, but driving in **TORONTO.**

7. Both hands in air, gesturing, both feet on accelerator, head turned to talk to person in back seat:
QUEBEC CITY.

8. One hand on 12 oz. double latte, one knee on wheel, cradling cellphone, foot on brake, banging head on steering wheel while stuck in traffic:
VANCOUVER.

9. One hand on wheel, one hand on hunting rifle, both feet on brake then both feet on accelerator - throwing McDonald's bag out the window:
FLIN FLON.

10. Four-wheel-drive pickup truck, shotgun mounted in rear window, beer cans on floor, joint in hand, raccoon tail attached to antenna:
PRINCE GEORGE.

11. Two hands gripping wheel, blue hair barely visible above windshield, driving at 40 kmh on Hwy 1 in the left lane with the left blinker on:
VICTORIA.

12. One Ski-Doo mitt on steering wheel, one Ski-Doo mitt out window scraping frost off windshield. Guess Who on eight-track playing Share The Land, hockey equipment stinking up car interior, waiting at lights for snow removal equipment to finish clearing inter-section:
WINNIPEG.

SPRINGTIME IN ALBERTA

When it's springtime in Alberta
And the gentle breezes blow,
About 100 kilometres an hour
And it's 30 degrees below.
You can tell you're in Alberta
'Cause the snow's up to your butt,
You take a breath of springtime air
And your nostrils both freeze shut.
The weather here is wonderful,
So I guess I'll hang around.
I could never leave Alberta
As my feet are frozen to the ground.

DIRTY TREE AND DIRTY TREE

An Alberta boss is interviewing a fellow from Quebec for a job.

"Question one," the foreman says. "Without using numbers, depict the number nine."

"Witout numbers?" the Quebecois asks. "Dat's easy," and he proceeds to draw three trees.

"What's this?" the boss asks.

" 'Ave you got no brain? Tree and tree and tree make nine."

"Fair enough," says the boss. "Question two. Same rules, but this time the number is 99."

The Quebecois picks up the picture he has just drawn and makes a smudge on each tree.

"Each of da trees is now dirty. So it's dirty tree, dirty tree, and dirty tree. Dat is 99."

"Last question," says the boss. "Same rules, and represent the number 100."

The Quebecer thinks a bit, picks up the picture and makes a little mark at the base of each tree.

" 'Ere you go. One 'undred."

"How does that represent 100?" asked the boss.

The Quebecois points to the marks at the tree bases.

"A dog come and does 'is business by each tree.

"Dirty tree and a turd, dirty tree and a turd, and dirty tree and a turd, which make one 'undred.

"When do I start?"

HAPPY CANADA DAY

A Canadian is someone who:

Thinks an income-tax refund is a gift from the government.

On seeing a light at the end of the tunnel, assumes it is an oncoming train.

Holds the world's record for telephone use, listening to "Don't hang up. Your call is important to us."

Is convinced democracy involves keeping your opinions to yourself.

In a restaurant, apologizes for not being ready to order at the waiter's convenience.

Travels across the border to buy cigarettes. Returns home for subsidized cancer therapy.

Says "sorry" when you accidentally bump into him.

Considers turning up the thermostat an integral part of foreplay.

Heartily proclaims, "Sure it's 30 C below. But it's a dry cold."

Spends an inordinate amount of time trying to define what a Canadian is.

AND THE WINNINGS ARE TAX-FREE

Did you hear about the $3,000,000 Saskatchewan Provincial Lottery?

The winner gets $3 a year for a million years.

WHISPER SWEET NOTHING

A Canadian goes to a Las Vegas house of ill repute.

A girl goes over to chat with him. They have a drink, start to snuggle. He whispers in her ear.

She gasps and runs away.

Seeing this, the madam sends over a more experienced lady.

Same thing. After a cuddle, he whispers in her ear. She screams "No!" and walks away.

The madam sends over Lola. Nothing would surprise Lola.

They frolic. He whispers in her ear. "No!" shouts Lola, louder than the other two. And she smacks him on the ear.

In all the years she's run brothels, the madame has never seen anything like this.

"What do you ask them," she inquires, "that makes them scream and run?"

"Not much," he replied. "Just if I could pay in Canadian dollars."

EVERYTHING'S BIGGER IN ALBERTA

A blind man decided to visit Alberta.

When he arrived, he sat in an oversized chair at the airport. "Wow, these seats are big!" he said.

"Yep," said the Albertan beside him. "Everything's big in Alberta."

He went to a pub in his hotel, ordered a beer.

The mug was placed between his hands.

"Wow," he said. "These mugs are big!"

"Yep," said the Albertan on the next bar stool. "Everything in Alberta is big."

After a couple of beers, the blind man asks where the washroom is.

He accidentally opens the wrong door, and falls into the hotel swimming pool.

Scared to death, the blind man starts shouting, "Don't flush! Don't flush!"

Gently Ethnic

POLISH HER NAILS

A Polish lad came to Canada and married a Canadian girl. Even though his English was far from perfect, they got on very well.

So the lawyer was surprised when the Polish man asked him to arrange a divorce, "very quick."

The lawyer sat the highly agitated man down, and started asking questions.

"Have you any grounds?"

"Ja, Ja," said the Pole. "An acre and half."

"Does your wife beat you up?"

"Never," he said. "I always up before her."

"So why do you want this divorce?"

"Because she going to kill me! I proof!"

"What kind of proof?" asks the lawyer.

"She buy bottle at drugstore, put on shelf in bathroom. I can read. It say 'Polish Remover.' "

ROUND FOR THE HOUSE

A Scotsman and an Irishman walk into a pub together.

The Scotsman yells, "A round for the house! It's on me!"

The next day the headlines read "Irish ventriloquist beaten behind pub."

ALL IN THE MILKING

How agri-corporations around the world would treat their cows.

NORTH AMERICAN CORPORATION: You have two cows. You sell one, and force the other to produce the milk of four cows. You are surprised when the cow drops dead.

FRENCH: You have two cows. You go on strike because you want three cows.

JAPANESE: You have two cows. You redesign them to 1/10 the size of ordinary cows, producing 20 times the milk. You then create clever cow cartoons called Cowkimon and market them worldwide.

GERMAN: You have two cows, re-engineered so they'll live for 100 years, eat once a month and milk themselves.

BRITISH: You have two cows. Both are mad.

RUSSIAN: You have two cows. You count them and learn you have five cows. You count them again and learn you have 42. You count them again and learn you have 12. You stop counting cows and open another bottle of vodka.

SWISS: You have 5,000 cows. None belongs to you. You charge others for storing them.

HINDU: You have two cows. You worship them.

CHINESE: You have two cows and 300 people milking them. You claim full employment, high bovine productivity and arrest the newsman who questions the numbers.

ELEMENTARY, MY DEAR WATSON

The Japanese eat a lot less fat and suffer fewer heart attacks than the British or Americans.

The French eat a lot more fat and also suffer fewer heart attacks than the British or Americans.

The Chinese drink very little red wine and suffer fewer heart attacks than the British or Americans.

The Italians drink excessive amounts of red wine and also suffer fewer heart attacks than the British or Americans.

Conclusion: Eat and drink what you like. It's speaking English that kills you.

TWO WONGS DON'T MAKE A WHITE

Su Wong marries Lee Wong.

The next year, the Wongs have a new baby.

The nurse brings them over a lovely, healthy, bouncy, but definitely Caucasian baby boy!

"Congratulations," says the nurse to the new parents. "What will you name the baby?"

The puzzled father looks at his new baby boy and says, "Well, two Wongs don't make a white, so I think we will name him Sum-Ting Wong."

A JOKE FOR ROBBIE BURNS DAY

A Scottish lad and lassie were gazing out over the loch.

"A penny for your thoughts Angus," she said shyly.

"I was thinkin'... perhaps it's aboot time for a wee kiss."

The girl blushed, kissed him on the cheek. The two turned again to gaze over the loch.

"Another penny for your thoughts, Angus."

"I was thinkin ... perhaps it's aboot time for a wee cuddle."

She blushed, leaned over and cuddled him for a few seconds. They gazed over the loch.

"Another penny for your thoughts, Angus."

"I was thinkin ... perhaps it's aboot time you let me poot ma hand on your leg."

She blushed, took his hand and put it on her knee. Then they gazed again over the loch.

Finally, the girl spoke again. "Another penny for your thoughts, Angus."

The young man knit his brow. "My thoughts are a bit more serious this time."

"Really?" said the girl in a whisper.

"Aye," said the lad. The girl looked away in shyness and bit her lip in anticipation of the ultimate request.

"Dinna ye think it's aboot time ye paid me the first three pennies?"

Billy Bob and Skeeter

A LITTLE LUMBER

Billy Bob was feeling guilty, so he went to confession.

"Father, I took a little lumber from a construction site."

"What did you do with the lumber, my son?" asked the priest.

"My porch had a hole. So I fixed it."

"That's not so bad."

"Well, Father, I had a little lumber left."

"What did you do with it?"

"Well, my dog needed a doghouse."

"Anything else?"

"Well, Father, I had a little lumber left. So, you know, I built a garage."

"Now this is getting a little out of hand."

"Well, Father, I had a little lumber left. My wife, she always wanted a bigger house. So I added two bedrooms and a new bathroom."

"That's definitely too much," said the priest. "For your penance you are going to have to make a novena. You do know how to make a novena, don't you?"

"No, Father, but if you've got the plans, I've got the lumber."

POOR CHOICE OF WORDS

"Doc," says Skeeter, "I want to be castrated."

"Are you absolutely sure?" asks the doc. "Once it's done, there's no going back. Your life will be forever changed."

"Doc, I've thought it through. Book me in to be castrated or I'll go to another doctor."

So Skeeter has his operation. The next day he is up and walking, slowly and painfully down the hospital corridor with his intravenous drip stand.

Heading towards him is another patient walking exactly the same way.

"Looks as if you've just had the same operation as me," says Skeeter.

"Oh yes," says the other patient, "I finally decided after 37 years of life that I would like to be circumcised."

Skeeter stares at him in horror. "Oh no," shrieks Skeeter, "THAT's the word!"

GREAT GIRTH

Billy Bob was standing next to a very fat fella at a urinal during a game.

For no discernible reason, the big guy leaned over and told Billy Bob he hadn't been able to see his privates for the past 15 years.

At a loss for words, not knowing what else to say, Billy Bob blurted out, "Why don't you diet?"

The fella gave Billy Bob a sideways stare.

"Dye it? What colour is it now?"

DON'T BRING UP THE MOTHER-IN-LAW

Billy Bob was on a vacation in Israel with his whole family, including his aged mother-in-law.

Wouldn't you know it - the mom-in-law up and dies in the middle of the trip.

Death certificate in hand, Billy Bob went to the Canadian Embassy to arrange to send her body back home.

Given the very expensive cost of transporting coffins, the ambassador offered the less-expensive option of burying the mom-in-law in the Holy Land.

"I don't care how much it costs," Billy Bob replied. "She's going back to Canada."

The ambassador was sympathetic. "You must have loved your mother-in-law very much, considering the difference in price."

"That's not it," said Billy Bob. "There was a case many years ago of a man buried here in Jerusalem.

"On the third day he arose from the dead.

"I can't take that chance with my mother-in-law!"

OF WHAT DOES HE SPEAK?

A cop pulled over Billy Bob for speeding.
"Have you any ID?" asked the cop.
"About what?" asked Billy Bob.

TRUCKIN' WITH BOBBY-SUE

Skeeter's walking along, when who pulls up but his pal Billy Bob in a new pick up truck.

Billy Bob's grinning to beat the band.

"Billy," asks Skeeter in wonderment. "Where'd ya get that truck?"

"Bobby-Sue give it to me," Billy Bob replies.

"She gave it to you? I know she's sweet on ya, but she gives you a brand-new truck?"

"Skeeter, listen up," says Billy Bob. "Me 'n' Bobby-Sue is out driving in the middle of nowhere. Bobby Sue pulls off the road, puts the truck into four-wheel drive, heads into the woods.

"She parks, gets out, throws off her clothes and says, 'Billy Bob, you can take whatever you want!'

"So ... I took the truck."

INSULTING TO WITCH DOCTORS

Billy Bob walks in the bar and orders two beers, "One for me, one for my best buddy."

"You want both now or do you want to wait for your friend?" asks the bartender.

"Both now," says Billy Bob. "I've got my best buddy in my pocket here."

And he pulls out an eight-centimetre-high man. "Wow!" says the barkeep. "He can drink a beer?"

"You bet. And then some." Sure enough, the little guy glugs down the beer.

"What else can he do? Can he walk?" Billy Bob flicks a loonie down the bar. "Hey Skeeter, go get that loonie." The little guy runs down, grabs the coin, brings it back.

"Amazing," says the barkeep. "What else? Does he talk?"

"Sure he talks. Skeeter, tell us about the time in Africa you insulted a witch doctor."

WHO'S ON CALL?

Billy Bob was leaving a well-known fishing lake with buckets of fish. He was stopped by a game warden.

"You're way over the limit with all these fish," the warden said.

"I'm not over any limit," replied Billy Bob. "These are my pet fish."

"Pet fish?!" the warden replied.

"Yup. Every night I take my pet fish down to this lake. I let 'em swim around for a while. Then I whistle. They jump back into the ice chests and I take them home."

"That's a bunch of hooey," scoffed the warden. "Fish can't do that."

"God's truth, my friend," said Billy Bob. "I'll show you. It really works."

Curiosity got the better of the game warden. "This I have to see," he muttered to himself.

Billy Bob poured the fish into the lake, stood and waited. After several minutes, the game warden turned to him and said, "Well?"

"Well, what?"

"When you going to call them back?" said the warden.

"Call who back?" said Billy Bob.

Spammed Again (Computers)

NEW VIRUS WARNING

If you receive an e-mail entitled "Badtimes," delete it immediately.

This one is nasty.

It will not only erase everything on your hard drive, but it will delete anything on disks within 10 metres of your computer.

It demagnetizes the strips on all your credit cards, re-programs your ATM access code, screws up the tracking on your VCR and uses subsonic harmonics to scratch any CDs you attempt to play.

It will rewrite your backup files, changing all active verbs to passive ones. It will incorporate subtle misspellings that will grossly change the interpretations of key sentences.

If the "Badtimes" message is opened in a Windows operating system, it will add antifreeze to your fish tank, flush the toilet while you shower, drink all your beer and leave dirty underwear under the coffee table.

Warn as many people as you can.

If you don't send this to 5,000 people in 20 seconds your right leg will spasm so hard it will give off sparks, igniting all nearby flammable materials.

In case you are blond, this is a joke.

MODERN LOVE STORY

Fella's on a Caribbean cruise when the boat sinks.

He ends up on an island, by himself, for four months.

A beautiful woman rows up to his beach. She was on the same island, on the other side. "How lucky, to have a rowboat wash up with you," he says.

"I made the rowboat myself," she says, "out of raw material on the island."

"But you had nothing to make it with."

"I found a strata of alluvial rock. I fired it in my kiln, it melted into ductile iron from which I forged my tools." The guy is stunned. They row back to her side of the island, up to an exquisite bungalow.

"Would you like to have a drink?" she says. "I have a still. Pina Colada?" After they talk, she says, "I'm slipping into something more comfortable. Why don't you shower and shave?"

In the bathroom is a razor made from a bone handle. Two shells honed to a hollow-ground edge are fastened on its end, inside a swivel mechanism. "What an amazing woman," he muses.

When he returns, she's wearing nothing but vines and a shell necklace. "We've been out here for a very long time," she purrs. "Is there something you've been longing for all these months?"

He can't believe what he's hearing. His heart begins to pound.

"You mean," he gasps, "I can check my e-mail from here?"

WHEN IN DOUBT, RE-BOOT

Three engineers - chemical, electrical and the third with Microsoft, are in a car.

The car stalls and stops by the side of the road.

The three engineers swap ideas about what could be wrong.

"Let's strip down the car's electronics," says the electrical engineer, "and trace back to where a fault might have occurred."

"Possibly the fuel has become emulsified," suggests the chemical engineer, "and is causing a blockage somewhere in the system."

"Why don't we close all the windows," says the Microsoft engineer, "get out, get back in, open the windows again, and maybe it will work."

MURPHY'S COMPUTING LAWS

• As soon as you delete a worthless file, you'll need it.

• Installing a new program will screw up at least one old one.

• The first place to look for a lost file is the last place you would expect to find it.

• Importat lettes that contin no erros will devlop rrors on the way to the priter.

• Regardless of the program, you won't have enough hard disk space to install it.

• The easier it is to get into a program, the harder it is to get out.

• The computer only crashes when you're working on a document you haven't saved.

• Whatever your computer-savvy friend fixed for you will always go wrong again ... when your friend is out of town.

CREATIVE USE OF THE INTERNET

Mom: "So how's your history paper coming?"

Son: "My professor suggested I use the Internet for research. It's been a great help."

Mom: "Really?"

Son: "Oh yes. So far I've located 17 people who will sell me one."

IF VEHICLES WERE LIKE COMPUTERS

For no reason whatsoever, your car would crash twice a day.

Occasionally, for no reason, your car would die on the freeway. You would have to stop, close all the windows, restart, and reopen the windows before continuing.

Occasionally, for no reason, a routine manoeuvre like a turn would cause the car to quit working. After hours of mechanical tinkering the only solution would be to reinstall the engine.

Only one person at a time could use the car.

Macintosh would make a car much faster and easier to drive than any other on the market. But it would only run on five per cent of the roads.

Occasionally, for no reason, your car would not let you in - unless you lifted the door handle, turned the key and grabbed hold of the antenna at the same time.

The car maker would require all buyers to purchase a deluxe set of road maps, even if they were neither needed nor desired. Trying to delete this option would cause the car's performance to diminish by 50% or more.

Every time a new car was introduced, the buyers would have to learn to drive all over again, because none of the controls would operate in the same manner as the old car.

What's the Hurry?

EVERY REACTION HAS AN ACTION

An old farmer had a lovely pond at the back of the farm. As he neared the pond one summer evening, he heard shouts and laughing.

A group of young women were skinny-dipping.

He immediately made his presence known. The girls swam to the deep end of the pond. One shouted, "We're not coming out until you leave!"

"I didn't come to see you ladies swim naked," he replied, "or to order you off my property.

"I only came to feed the alligators."

PEDESTRIAN QUESTION

Fella's driving through Ireland on holiday.

He stops for a break at a pleasant country pub.

While enjoying a leisurely pint of Guinness, he chats to Mick the barman. "By the way," he says, "can you tell me the quickest way to Dublin?"

"Are you walking or driving?" asks Mick.

"Driving," says the tourist.

"Ah, well," says Mick. "That's definitely the quickest way."

HIGH PRIORITY

Fella calls the police in the middle of the night.

"Somebody's in my shed stealing things."

"Sorry, sir," said the dispatcher, "nobody's in your area, but we'll send over an officer as soon as possible."

A minute later, the fella calls 911 again.

"Hi there," he says. "I called you a minute ago because there were people in my shed.

"You don't have to hurry now, because I've shot them."

Within minutes, half a dozen police cars surround his house, plus helicopters and a SWAT unit. They catch the burglars red-handed.

"I thought you said you'd shot them," said a policeman.

"I thought you said no one was available," he replied.

NOT THAT THINGS HAVE BEEN SLOW LATELY

What'd the snail say as it rode on the tortoise's back?

Whee!

SPEED UP

Why did the city employee step on the snail?

Darned thing had followed him around all morning.

Very Punny

ANIMALS ARE EXPENSIVE

A woman brought a limp parrot to the vet.

"I'm sorry," said the vet, laying the bird down on his examination table. "This parrot is dead."

"Are you sure?" wailed the owner. "Might he be in a coma? Isn't there anything you can do?"

The vet retrieved a black Labrador.

The dog stood on his hind legs, sniffed the lifeless parrot from beak to tail, shook its head and barked.

The vet took away the dog, returned with a cat.

The cat delicately sniffed the bird, shook its head and meowed.

"Like I said," said the vet to the women. "Your parrot is definitely not alive."

He then produced a bill.

"What?" exclaimed the woman, "$150 just to tell me my bird is dead. That's ridiculous!"

"If you had believed me," the vet said, "the bill would be $20. But with the Lab report and the Cat scan ... "

EAT UP THE NEWS

A captive was brought before the cannibal chief.

"And what is your profession?" the chief asked.

The man replied, "I am an editor for The Edmonton Sun."

"Good," smiled the cannibal chief. "Tomorrow you will be editor-in-chief."

TECHNICOLOUR MEMORIES

Jack hadn't been to a class reunion in decades.

When he walked into this latest one, he thought he recognized a woman over in the corner, so he approached her and extended his hand in greeting, saying, "You look like Helen Brown."

"Well," the woman snapped back, "You don't look so great in blue either!"

WHAT DOES SHE SELL BY THE SEASHORE?

A couple on a southern holiday noticed a girl walking along the beach with a bag.

She kept approaching sunbathers, glancing around, then speaking to them.

Occasionally someone would nod.

There would be an exchange of money and something taken from her bag.

The couple assumed she was selling drugs. They continued to watch her for weeks.

The wife noticed the girl was only approaching people with portable stereos.

Intrigued to the point of obsession, she asked her husband to lie on the beach the next day with a boom box while she watched from their hotel balcony.

The plan went without a hitch. The wife was beside herself with anticipation when the girl walked up to talk to her husband.

"Well," she squealed when her husband returned to the room, "is she a drug-dealer?"

"No," said her husband, "she's a battery salesperson."

"A what?" exclaimed the wife.

"A battery salesperson," he said. "She sells C cells by the seashore."

SWEET TOOTH

Chirped a robin on the ground to a robin flying by:
"Come on down. The worms here are delicious."

The other robin did.

The duo gorged themselves.

The weather was warm, the sun was shining.

The little fellas, so stuffed, fell asleep on the ground.

Along came a hungry cat, delighted to find his afternoon snack with such little effort.

Licking his chops as he left the scene of the crime, the cat said to himself: "I sure do love Baskin' robins!"

SOMETHING FISHY

Two parrots were sitting on a perch.

"Hey," said one to the other. "I think I smell a fish."

Jokes For Special Days

STAR WARS CHRISTMAS

Darth Vader and Luke Skywalker were having one of their father-and-son chats - light sabers drawn, sparks flying.

Vader pinned Luke against a wall and wheezed into his face.

"I know what you're getting for Christmas, Luke."

Luke fought free. "That's impossible!" he cried. "How could you know what I'm getting for Christmas?"

Darth Vader shot Luke an icy glare:

"I felt your presents."

STAGES OF LIFE AS DEFINED AT CHRISTMASTIME

You believe in Santa Claus.
You don't believe in Santa Claus.
You are Santa Claus.
You look like Santa Claus.

NEW YEAR'S WISHES

May you get a clean bill of health from your dentist, cardiologist, gastro-enterologist, urologist, proctologist, podiatrist, psychiatrist, plumber and Tax Canada.

May your hair, teeth, facelift, hips, abs and stocks not fall.

May your blood pressure, triglycerides, cholesterol, white blood count and mortgage interest rates not rise.

May what you see in the mirror delight you. May what others see in you delight them. May someone love you enough to forgive your faults, be blind to your blemishes, and tell the world about your virtues.

May the telemarketers make their sales calls when you're not in the bathtub. May the commercials on TV not be louder than the program being watched.

May your chequebook and budget balance, with generous amounts for charity.

May you remember to say "I love you" at least once a day to your spouse, child, parents and siblings; not to your secretary, masseur, hairdresser or fitness instructor.

May we live in a world at peace and with the awareness of God's love in every sunset, every baby's smile, every lover's kiss, and every wonderful, astonishing, miraculous beat of our hearts.

VALENTINE'S DAY

Valentine's: A day when you have dreams of a candlelight dinner, diamonds, and romance, but consider yourself lucky to get a card.

A new women's organization wants to pay their own way on dates, doesn't expect roses and chocolates on Valentine's and doesn't want men to hold open the door. It's called "Women's Fib."

TOASTS FOR ST. PATRICK'S DAY

"Let's raise a glass to Irish potatoes and drink till our noses look like tomatoes."

"If in heaven we do not meet, I'll bang on the pipes 'til you send up some heat."

"May the good saints protect you, the devil neglect you."

"If you slide down the banister of life, may the splinters point in the right direction."

"May the wind always be at your back. And may you be somewhere else should the wind come from someone else's back!"

LUCK OF THE IRISH – ST. PATRICK'S DAY

Patrick O'Reilly is walking along some railroad tracks.

His foot gets stuck.

He hears a noise and turns to see a train off in the distance.

Panicking, he starts to pray.

"God, please get my foot out of these tracks. I'll stop drinking."

Nothing happened. The train was getting closer.

He prayed again, "God, get my foot out. I'll stop drinking AND cussing."

Still nothing. The train was seconds away.

Patrick tried one more time, "Lord, pleeeeeze. If you get my foot out of the tracks, I'll quit drinking, cussing, smoking and fooling around with sinful women."

Suddenly his foot shot out of the tracks. He dived out of the way, just in time as the train whistled by.

Patrick got up, dusted himself off and looked toward Heaven.

"Thanks anyway God," he said, "but I managed to get it out myself."

EASTER IN CANADA

You know you're in Canada when ...

You went Easter-egg hunting in the blizzard.

Rather than taking your long underwear off for the season, you put another pair on.

Turning up the thermostat has become an integral part of foreplay.

Upon exploratory groping with one's mate, you shout "eureka!" when skin is discovered under all those layers of nightclothes.

You found the Easter Bunny frozen under a snow-drift.

Four seasons have blended into one: winter, winter, winter and still winter.

THANKSGIVING TURKEY JOKE

The lady was picking through the frozen turkeys at the grocery store, but couldn't find one big enough for her family.

"Do these turkeys get any bigger," she asked the stock boy.

"No ma'am," he replied. "They're dead."

HALLOWEEN MONSTER MASH

What happened to the monster children who ate all their vegetables?
They gruesome.

What would you do if a witch, an alien, Count Dracula and Frankenstein showed up at your door?
Hope it's Halloween.

What did the monster eat after the dentist pulled his tooth?
The dentist!

Why did the vampire subscribe to the newspaper?
He heard it had great circulation.

SIGNS YOU'RE TOO OLD TO TRICK-OR-TREAT

You get winded from knocking on the door.
You ask a kid to chew the candy for you.
You ask for high-fibre candy only.
When someone drops a candy bar in your bag, you lose your balance and fall over.
People say, "Great Keith Richards mask!" and you're not wearing one.
When the door opens you yell, "Trick or ..." and danged if you can remember the rest.
By the end of the night, you have a bag full of restraining orders.
You have to carefully choose a costume that won't dislodge your hairpiece.
You're the only superhero in the neighbourhood with a walker.
You avoid houses where your ex-wives live.

All Creatures Great And Small (Animals)

SWEET AND STICK

Mama mole, papa mole and baby mole all live in a little mole hole.

One day papa mole sticks his head out of the hole, sniffs the air and says, "Yum! I smell maple syrup!"

Mama mole sticks her head out of the hole, sniffs, and says, "Yum! I smell honey!"

Baby mole tries to stick his head out of the hole to sniff the air, but can't because the bigger moles are in the way.

"Geez," says the baby mole. "All I can smell is … molasses!"

DOG'S LIFE

A police officer is parking his van in front of the station.

In the back, his canine partner Jake starts barking at a little boy.

"Is that a dog you got back there?" the little boy asks.

"It sure is," the officer replies.

Puzzled, the boy looks at the policeman, and back at the van.

Finally the little fella asks: "What'd he do that was so bad?"

CANINE BULB TURNERS

How many dogs does it take to change a light bulb?

Labrador: Oh, me, me!!!! Pleeeeeeeeeeeeeze let me change the light bulb! Can I? Can I? Huh? Huh? Huh? Can I???

Jack Russell terrier: I'll pop it in while I bounce off the walls.

Poodle: I'll just blow in the border collie's ear and he'll do it. By the time he rewires the house, my nails will be dry.

German shepherd: Everyone stop where you are! Who busted the light? I SAID "STOP WHERE YOU ARE!!!"

Cocker spaniel: Why change it? I'll pee on the carpet in the dark.

Australian cattle dog: First, I'll put the light bulbs in a circle ...

Dachshund: You know I can't reach that stupid lamp!

English sheep dog: Light bulb? Sorry, I don't see a light bulb.

Mastiff: Mastiffs are NOT afraid of the dark.

Chihuahua: Yo quiero Taco Bulb.

Pointer: I see it, there it is, there it is, right there ...

Greyhound: It isn't moving. Who cares?

Rottweiler: Make me.

BATTERED BAT

A young vampire bat flaps into the cave covered in fresh blood.

He settles on the cave ceiling to get some sleep. The other bats smell the blood and start hassling him about where he got so lucky.

"OK!" he finally says. "If I show you, will you let me sleep?"

Hundreds of bats follow him out the cave, through the valley and into the deep forest.

Finally he slows down. All the other bats excitedly fly tight around him.

"See that tree over there?" he asks.

"Yes, yes, yes!" the bats all scream in a frenzy.

"Good," he says, "because I DIDN'T!"

FATAL RETRACTION

Fellow comes out of his house to see his dog running around with the neighbour's pet rabbit in his mouth. The rabbit is dead.

He panics, thinking the dog has started the Third World War with the neighbour. He brings the dirty, chewed-up rabbit in the house, bathes it, blow-dries its fur. Sneaking next door, he puts the rabbit back in its cage, hoping the neighbours will think it died of natural causes.

Days later, the neighbour comes over. "Did the kids tell you Fluffy died last week?"

The guy fakes it. "No! What happened?"

"The weirdest thing," replies the neighbour.

"We just found Fluffy dead in his cage. But the day after we buried him, somebody dug him up, gave him a bath and put him back into the cage.

"What kind of a wacko would do that?"

ALL THE WAY HOME

The three little pigs go out for dinner.

The waiter comes and takes their drink order. The first two ask for pop.

"Water for me," says the third. "Lots and lots of water."

The drinks are brought out and the waiter takes their orders. A steak for the first, a salad for the second. "I want water," said the third. "Lots and lots of water."

When it came to desserts, the first piggy wanted a banana split, the second a root beer float. But the third just said, "Water. Lots and lots of water."

"Pardon me for asking," said the waiter, "but why have you ordered nothing but water?"

"Well," said the third piggy, "somebody has to go wee, wee, wee, all the way home!"

DON'T ASK THE ELEPHANT

The lion is strutting through the jungle. He comes upon a chipmunk. "Who's the king of the jungle?" he roars. "Y-y-you are," stammers the chipmunk.

Satisfied, the lion moseys on. He meets a monkey. "Who's the king of the jungle?" he roars again. "You are, you are, you are," chatters the monkey.

In a clearing, the lion sees an elephant. He gives the elephant a swipe on the trunk to get his attention. "Who's the king of the jungle?"

The elephant looks at the lion, grabs him with his trunk, hoists him in the air, slams him to the ground, stomps on the lion for good measure and moves on.

The lion, black and blue and unable to move, yells after the elephant.

"Just because you don't know the answer doesn't mean you should get so mad!!!"

I Think I Can,
I Know I Can
(Positive Thinking)

A fella arrives with his resume for an interview.

The personnel officer scans his employment record.

"I must say your work history is terrible," the potential employer says. "You've been fired from every job you've ever held."

"Yes," replies the man.

"Well, there's not much positive in that," says the officer.

"Hey!" says the guy, poking at his application. "At least I'm not a quitter!"

HOW TO SUCCEED IN THIS LIFE

A little boy was talking to himself, wearing his baseball cap and toting a ball and bat:

"I'm the greatest hitter in the world," he announced.

He tossed the ball into the air, swung at it and missed. "Strike one!" he yelled.

Undaunted, he picked up the ball and said again, "I'm the greatest hitter in the world!"

He tossed the ball into the air.

When it came down he swung again and missed. "Strike two!" he cried.

The boy examined his bat and ball, spit on his hands and rubbed them together. He straightened his cap and said once more, "I'm the greatest hitter in the world!"

Again he tossed the ball up in the air and swung at it. He missed. "Strike three!

"Wow!" he exclaimed. "I'm the greatest pitcher in the world!!"

From The Heart (Sentimental Thoughts)

YES, VIRGINIA, THERE ARE MANY 'WIVES OF GOD'

A little boy about 10 years old was in front of the shoe store, bare foot, intently peering through the window and shivering with cold.

A lady approached the boy. "Young man, why are you looking so hard at that window?"

"I was asking God to give me a pair of shoes," was the boy's reply.

The lady took him by the hand and went into the store.

She asked the clerk to get half a dozen pairs of socks for the boy.

She took the lad to the washroom, washed his little feet. The clerk having brought the socks, she placed a pair on the boy's feet and then purchased him a pair of shoes.

She packaged the remaining pairs of socks and gave them to him.

The lad caught her by the hand.

Looking up at her with tears in his eyes, he asked, "Are you God's wife?"

WHEN YOU THOUGHT I WASN'T LOOKING

When you thought I wasn't looking ... I saw you hang my first painting on the refrigerator, and I immediately wanted to paint another one.

I saw you feed a stray cat, and I learned it was good to be kind to animals.

I saw you making my favourite cake for me and I learned that the little things can be the special things in life.

I heard you say a prayer, and I knew there is a god I could always talk to and I learned to trust in God.

I saw you make a meal and take it to a friend who was sick, and I learned that we all have to help take care of each other.

I saw you give of your time and money to help people who had nothing and I learned that those who have something should give to those who don't.

I felt you kiss me good night and I felt loved and safe.

I saw you take care of our house and every one in it and I learned we have to take care of what we are given.

I saw how you handled your responsibilities, even when you didn't feel good and I learned that I would have to be responsible when I grow up.

I saw tears come from your eyes and I learned that sometimes things hurt, but it's alright to cry.

I saw that you cared and I wanted to be everything that I could be.

I learned most of life's lessons that I need to know to be a good and productive person when I grow up.

SEVEN WONDERS OF THE WORLD

A class was asked to list what the students thought were the present Seven Wonders of the World. Though there was some disagreement, the following got the most votes:

1. Egypt's Great Pyramids; 2. Taj Mahal; 3. Grand Canyon; 4. Panama Canal; 5. Empire State Building; 6. St. Peter's Basilica; 7. China's Great Wall.

While gathering the votes, the teacher noticed one student hadn't turned in her paper.

She asked the girl if she was having trouble with her list.

"Yes," replied the girl. "I couldn't quite make up my mind. There were so many."

The teacher said, "Well, tell us what you have, and maybe we can help."

The student replied: "I think the Seven Wonders of the World are: 1. To touch; 2. To taste; 3. To see; 4. To hear; 5. To feel; 6. To laugh; 7. To love."

LOVE OF A CHILD

A man punished his four-year-old daughter for wasting a roll of gold wrapping paper.

Money was tight and he was angry when the child tried to decorate a box to put under the Christmas tree.

Nevertheless, the little girl brought the gift to her father the next morning and said, "This is for you, Daddy."

He was embarrassed by his earlier overreaction, but his anger flared again when he found the box was empty. He yelled at her, "Don't you know when you give someone a present, there's supposed to be something inside it?"

The little girl looked up at him with tears in her eyes and said, "Daddy, it's not empty. I blew kisses into the box. All for you, Daddy."

The father was crushed. He hugged his little girl, begged for her forgiveness.

An accident took the life of the child only a short time later.

The man kept that gold box by his bed for years. Whenever he was discouraged (or coping with that temper of his), he would take out an imaginary kiss and remember the love of the child who had put it there.

TENDER MERCIES

Be thankful for ...

The spouse who hogs the covers every night, because he/she is not out with someone else.

The teenager who is lying around watching TV. He/she is at home and not on the streets.

For the taxes we pay. It means we're employed.

For the mess after a party. We have been surrounded by friends.

For too-snug clothing. We have enough to eat.

For snow that needs shovelling and windows that need cleaning. We have a home.

For all the complaining about the government. We have freedom of speech.

For the parking spot way off at the end of the parking lot. We can walk. We have a car.

For our huge heating bill. We are warm.

For the lady in church who sings off key. We can hear.

For the unending pile of laundry. We have clothing.

For the early morning alarm. It means we're alive.

And finally ...

For too much e-mail. Our friends are thinking of us.